His Daughters

"Leaning and Depending on the Lord"

My comfort in my suffering is this:
Your promise preserves my life.

Psalm 119:50(NIV)

His Daughters

"Leaning and Depending on the Lord"

Bonita L. Williams

Vision Inspired Publications
Atlanta, Georgia

His Daughters

"Leaning and Depending on the Lord"

Copyright © 2013 by Bonita L. Williams
Published by Vision Inspired Publications
Atlanta, Georgia
Revised 2022

Trust GOD from the bottom of your heart;
don't try to figure out everything on your own.
Listen for GOD's voice in everything you do,
everywhere you go;
he's the one who will keep you on track.

Proverbs 3:5-6 (MSG)

ISBN: 978-0-9856187-1-1

Printed in the United States of America

His Daughters

"Leaning and Depending on the Lord"

Do not conform to the pattern of this world but be transformed by the renewing of your mind. Then you will be able to test and approve what God's will is—his good, pleasing and perfect will.

Romans 12:2 (NIV)

Dedication

This book is dedicated to my mother in love Myrtle Dansby (Little Mama), whose open heart has been an encouragement to many people.

Therefore, if anyone is in Christ, he is a new creature; the old things passed away; behold, new things have come.

2 Corinthians 5:17 (NASB)

Acknowledgments

Special thanks to all my sisters in Christ who have been there for me over the years.
Thank You! Thank You! Thank You!

Scarlette, thank you for your sisterhood, love, and support throughout the years.

Dianna, thank you for the spirit of love you have always shared with me.

Gwen, thank God that He has allowed us to weather the storms together.

Evelyn, thank you for accepting the job assignment of being Benecia's Godmother and much more.

Peggy, thanks to you for your wonderful support throughout the years.

Dianne, thanks for our special connection.

Dorcas, thanks for sharing your creative genius with me.

Marian, thanks for being my walking partner in more ways than one.

Sandra, thank you for the kindness you always shower me with.

Regina, thanks to you for your giving spirit which always encourages me.

Jacqueline, thanks for being a sounding board through all my writing ventures.

Marsha, thanks for sharing your wonderful smile and pleasant spirit with me throughout the years.

Jackie **D,** thanks to you for being a role model in the service of our Heavenly Father.

Brenda, thanks to you for sharing your mom with me.

To each of you I say thank you for all the love, well wishes, help, tissues, pats on the back, hand holding and all the rest of the things you do to enrich my life.

But blessed is the one who trusts in the LORD,
whose confidence is in him.
Jeremiah 17:7 (NIV)

CONTENTS

So, chosen by God for this new life of love, dress in the wardrobe God picked out for you: compassion, kindness, humility, quiet strength, discipline. Be even-tempered, content with second place, quick to forgive an offense. Forgive as quickly and completely as the Master forgave you. And regardless of what else you put on, wear love. It's your basic, all-purpose garment. Never be without it.

Colossians 3:12-14 (MSG)

INTRODUCTION

One of my favorite passages in God's Word is Proverbs 3:5-6.

Trust in the LORD with all thine heart; and lean not unto

thine own understanding.

In all thy ways acknowledge him, and he shall direct thy paths. Proverbs 3:5-6 (KJV)

As children of God, we have been given the wonderful privilege of being able to have an intimate relationship with our Heavenly Father. God is always just a prayer away. The Holy Spirit is with us 24 hours a day, 7 days a week to lead and guide us.

Our part in all of this is to trust God. God knows exactly what He is doing. Jeremiah 29:11 tells us that God has plans for us. In order to experience the pure joy God has for us we must be willing to trust and obey Him.

His Daughters is an opportunity for us to daily surrender our will to God and receive the blessings God has for us. God's Word is full of promises for all of us. ***His Daughters*** takes a look at ten (10) of those promises. As you read through each promise ask the Holy Spirit to speak to your heart.

Claim Checks are used to retrieve items that belong to us. God's promises belong to His children. There is a section after each promise entitled "Claim Check". Take time to claim the promises listed in the book. Your message can take the form of a letter, prayer, song or any format that you are led to use.

Bonita L. Williams

Whereby are given unto us exceeding great and precious promises: that by these ye might be partakers of the divine nature, having escaped the corruption that is in the world through lust.

2 Peter 1:4(KJV)

UP! UP! And AWAY!

Dear Daughters,

"Peace, I give to you, my peace I give to you". The peace of God truly surpasses man's understanding. In a world full of turmoil how can one expect to have peace? Every day the television and newspaper reports are full of doom and gloom. Destruction seems to be the plan. What steps can we take to experience the promise of peace God gave to us? There is only one answer, JESUS! Turning to the Lord in time of trouble allows the believer in Christ an opportunity to rest on His promises. Not only will He give you peace when things are going well, He'll give you peace during your storms.

When we allow our faith to rise upward our fears will fly away. God's peace is yours for the asking. Let go and let God handle everything. Our fears can be blown away when we take the following actions:

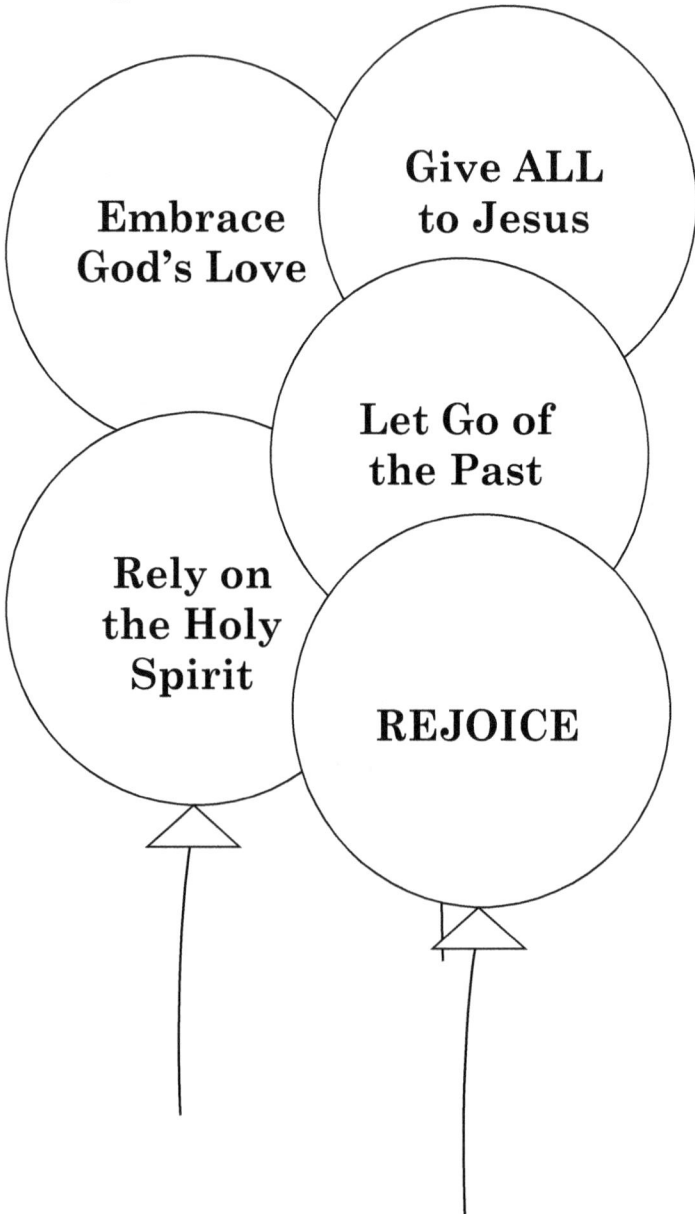

Embrace God's Love

Give ALL to Jesus

Let Go of the Past

Rely on the Holy Spirit

REJOICE

Once we realize what has already been done for us, we are able to release our fears and they will be up, up, and away. The peace of God which passes all understanding is already within us as a part of the fruit of the Holy Spirit.

THE PROMISE

Fear thou not; for I am with thee: be not dismayed; for I am thy God: I will strengthen thee; yea, I will help thee; yea, I will uphold thee with the right hand of my righteousness.
Isaiah 41:10(KJV)

Isaiah 41:10 is a scripture God directed me to many years ago. This passage has given me many years of comfort.

Let's take a close look at the passage.

Fear thou not; for I am with thee: be not dismayed; for I am thy God: I will strengthen thee; yea, I will help thee; yea, I will uphold thee with the right hand of my righteousness. Isaiah 41:10(KJV)

The first part of the scripture tells us to:

FEAR NOT

That sounds like a command to me.

FEAR THOU NOT

Fear leads to despair, frustration, turmoil, sickness, and distress.

FEAR has been described as…

False
Evidence
Appearing
Real

Believing the lies of the enemy (satan) can lead to **fear.** Instead of becoming fearful we should remember why we don't have to fear.

<u>We don't have to fear because God is with us.</u>

Take a few minutes to think of times when God might **not** be with us.

The truth is that God is always with us.

Fear not for I am with you….

Each day we need to realize who is with us. <u>God is always with us.</u>

He is our God. The God who created Heaven and earth is with us. The owner of the cattle on a thousand hills is with us. The alpha and omega is with us.

GOD IS WITH US

What does God promise to do for us in Isaiah 41:10?

???

He promises to:

STRENGTHEN US

HELP US

WOW!

Strength from the Lord!

Help from the Lord!

Not only will He be help and strength for us He also promises to hold us up with His right hand of righteousness.

That means that He's got our backs. The enemy can do nothing to us.

Based on the message from Isaiah 41:10 what should we do when Satan tries to steal our peace.

- **FEAR NOT**

- **REMEMBER WHO IS WITH US (GOD)**

- **REMEMBER WHERE OUR STRENGTH AND HELP COMES FROM(GOD)**

- **REST IN THE ARMS OF OUR HEAVENLY FATHER**

Claim Check

Write a personal message to God about His promise to you.

Send me your light and your faithful care,
let them lead me;
let them bring me to your holy mountain,
to the place where you dwell.

Psalm 43:3 (NIV)

FREEZE

Dear Daughters,

There is a children's game where children run toward a caller. The children run until the caller says 1, 2, 3 RED Light. Then the children freeze and wait for the caller to turn around again. There are many times when it seems as if God is saying, "1, 2, 3, freeze. Stop dead in your tracks. Stop running the way you are going." God puts red lights in our lives to give us an opportunity to look at where we are. We are given time to see how we are travelling. Are we going in the direction God has planned for us? FREEZE! Look at what's going on. Are we spending enough time in God's Word? Have we forgotten what Jesus did for us? Are we trying to depend upon ourselves? STOP! Take inventory. Ask for God's guidance. God knows the plans He has for us (Jeremiah 29:11). He expects us to follow the road map He has for our lives. We should remind ourselves that God knew us before the foundation of the world.

Blessed be the God and Father of our Lord Jesus Christ, who has blessed us with every spiritual blessing in the heavenly places in Christ, just as He chose us in Him before the foundation of the world, that we would be holy and blameless before Him. In love He predestined us to adoption as sons through Jesus Christ to Himself, according to the kind intention of His will.

Ephesians 1:3-5

THE PROMISE

I will instruct thee and teach thee in the way which thou shalt go I will guide thee with mine eye.
Psalm 32:8 (KJV)

To receive God's guidance, we must spend time:

Praying

Reading God's Word

Listening to the Holy Spirit

Whatever is happening in your life right now?

FREEZE!!!

Ask God to lead and guide you in the way you should go.

Look at your activities for the last few days.

How much time did you spend in the following activities?

E-mailing

Texting

Talking on the phone

Watching television

Shopping

Reading something other than God's Word

Praying to God

Reading God's Word

Meditating on God's Word

Memorizing God's Word

Encouraging someone

If the time spent with anything other than focusing on God is greater than being with your very best friend, Jesus, perhaps some changes need to be made.

David was described as a man after God's own heart. Why was this phrase used? David had learned to lean and depend on the Lord. Yes, he made some mistakes, but he remembered where his true help came from. To become a woman after God's heart we have to spend time with God. We are told to "seek ye first the kingdom of God." The word "seek" means to look for. Daily we are to look for God in everything we do. No decisions should be made without seeking God's will.

Daily ask God for wisdom, knowledge and understanding.

Be still and know that God is GOD.

*We should always allow God to show us **His** ways and to teach us **His** paths for our lives.*

Claim Check

Write a personal message to God about His promise to you.

For we are His workmanship, created in Christ Jesus for good works, which God prepared beforehand so that we would walk in them.

Ephesians 2:10 (NASB)

SLIPPING VS FALLING

Dear Daughters,

Many situations of life cause us to slip in our Christian walk with God. The hustle and bustle of life often causes us to slip away from things that are important to our spiritual growth. We might slip away from our devotional time. We might be too busy to take time to pray without ceasing. We might slip in our giving because we feel that we cannot afford to tithe. Perhaps we forget that the money belongs to God. We might slip in our stewardship of time because we have too much to do. Hair appointments must be kept. Our nails need to be manicured. Shopping for that special outfit must take place. That favorite TV program just can't be missed. How can one balance all these things?

Days just don't hold enough hours. There's not enough time to visit the sick or participate in church activities. We might slip in our fellowship with other believers. We just want to keep to ourselves. Spending time at church other than on Sunday just can't be done. With all this slipping and sliding how can we truly be the person God intends for us to be? How can we stop slipping?

First we must remember that we may slip and slide but we will never fall from God's grace. In the book of Jude, it states that Jesus is able to keep us from falling. The way to stop slipping is to commit our lives to Christ and trust Him to order our steps. Trust Him to shine a light on our paths. Though life might be slippery, we should keep our eyes on Jesus. He can and will keep us from falling.

THE PROMISE

The LORD makes firm the steps of the one who delights in him; though he may stumble, he will not fall, for the LORD upholds him with his hand.
Psalm 37:23-24 (NIV)

Scheduling time with God is essential in our walk with Jesus.

WALKING WITH JESUS

The **WALK** with Jesus is a joy that words cannot explain.

Willingly obey the commands of God.
Read John 14:21

Allow God to guide you through each day.
Read 1 Peter 5:7

Let God have every area of your life.
Read Gal 5:16-17, Acts 1:8

Keep your mind on Jesus throughout every day.
Read: Acts 17:11, Colossians 1:27, Revelation 3:20

Always walk in the Spirit of God.

Claim Check

Write a personal message to God about His promise to you.

*I have come into the world as a light, so
that no one who believes in me should stay
in darkness.*
John 12:46 (NIV)

THE WINNERS CIRCLE

Dear Daughters,

Many people fail to enjoy the abundant life that Jesus wants us to experience. Some people feel that the wonderful blessings of the Lord are just too good to be true. They can't enjoy the mountain top experiences for looking for the valley ones. "This is just too good to be true." "This just can't last." "Now is not the time for this." "I know the bomb is going to hit anytime now." Oh, ye of little faith. Rejoice and be glad every day the Lord sends your way. Don't spend time in fear and doubt. Spend time resting in the green pastures of life, remembering that the Lord is truly your shepherd. Allow the wonderful peace of God to engulf your total being. Don't dwell on the negative. We have been given the present time as our gift from the Lord. The past is gone and should be laid to rest. The future is not a reality yet. What we have is the here and now. Get rid your loser mentality. Enjoy the winners circle by remembering that God sent His Son into the world to redeem your soul. You won when you accepted Christ as your Lord and Savior.

THE PROMISE

That if thou shalt confess with thy mouth the Lord Jesus, and shalt believe in thine heart that God hath raised him from the dead, thou shalt be saved.

Romans 10:9(KJV)

Salvation is ours for the asking through Jesus.

There is nothing we can do to be saved.

Salvation is free.

Look at the scripture below:

Romans 10:9

The Message (MSG)

[4-10]The earlier revelation was intended simply to get us ready for the Messiah, who then puts everything right for those who trust him to do it. Moses wrote that anyone who insists on using the law code to live right before God soon discovers it's not so easy—every detail of life regulated by fine print! But trusting God to shape the right living in us is a different story— no precarious climb up to heaven to recruit the Messiah, no dangerous descent into hell to rescue the Messiah. So, what exactly was Moses saying?

The word that saves is right here,
as near as the tongue in your mouth,
as close as the heart in your chest.
It's the word of faith that welcomes God to go to work and set things right for us. This is the core of our preaching. Say the welcoming word to God—"Jesus is my Master"—

embracing, body and soul, God's work of doing in us what he did in raising Jesus from the dead. That's it. You're not "doing" anything; you're simply calling out to God, trusting him to do it for you. That's salvation. With your whole being you embrace God setting things right, and then you say it, right out loud: "God has set everything right between him and me!"

Jesus' death, burial and resurrection put us in right relationship with our Heavenly Father.

Complete the passages below. All the scriptures are from the King James Bible.

Romans 10:13

For whosoever shall _____ upon the name of the _____ shall be _____.

John 3:16

For God so loved the_____, that he gave his only

begotten_____, that whosoever _____ in him

should not_____ but have _____ life.

John 1: 12

But as many as_____ him, to them gave ____

power to become the sons of _____, even to

them that believe on his_____.

Romans 4:8

_____ is the man to whom the_____

will not _____ sin.

Our sins are <u>not</u> counted against us by the Lord. We are forgiven by the grace of God.

As children of God, we can rejoice that we are now able to have a truly intimate relationship with Him.

Claim
Check

Write a personal message to God about
His promise to you.

For by grace are ye saved through faith; and that not of yourselves: it is the gift of God: Not of works, lest any man should boast.
Ephesians 2:8-9(KJV)

ETCHED IN STONE / SUBJECT TO CHANGE

Dear Daughters,

The statement has been made that nothing is constant but change. How we handle change depends on our relationship with God. If we realize that God can handle any changes in our lives, then we continue to have peace; it's when the unexpected happens and we don't turn to God we experience frustrations. Life can be full of uncertainties. People and things we count on can disappoint us. Plans can go haywire. People we thought were the rocks of Gibraltar can tumble down, but we can take comfort in the Rock of ages (Jesus).

God's love for us is etched in stone. His Word states that nothing shall separate us from His love. No situation too difficult! No trial too hard! No way too dark! Regardless of the changes in our lives we can count on God.

THE PROMISE

Nay, in all these things we are more than
conquerors through him that loved us.
For I am persuaded, that neither death,
nor life, nor angels, nor principalities,
nor powers, nor things present, nor things
to come. Nor height, nor depth, nor any
other creature, shall be able to separate
us from the love of God, which is
in Christ Jesus our Lord.
Romans 8:37-39 (KJV)

FACTS TO REMEMBER

God is on our side.

God didn't hesitate to put everything on the line for us, He sent His own Son to die for us.

No one who dares tangle with God's chosen will succeed.

Nothing or no one can drive a wedge between us and the love that Christ's has for us:

Not trouble

Not hard times

Not hatred

Not hunger

Not homelessness

Not bullying threats

Not backstabbing

Not sickness

Not backsliding

Not wealth or poverty

Nothing living or dead

Angelic or demonic

Today or tomorrow

Highs or lows

Up or down

Ins or outs

Thinkable or unthinkable—

Absolutely- positively nothing can get

between us and God's love for us because

of the sacrifice made on the cross by Jesus

Christ.

Claim Check

Write a personal message to God about His promise to you.

Trust in the LORD forever,
For in GOD the LORD, we have an
everlasting Rock.
Isaiah 26:4

A BREATH OF FRESH AIR

Dear Daughters,

Feeling upside down, hassled, hurried, exhausted? Well take a deep breath! That's it, go right ahead and breathe. One more time, inhale in the blessings of the Lord, exhale all the worry, doubt, and fear. You should be feeling a little bit better now. Most of us forget to breathe. Yes, we use God's air every second of every day and we take it for granted. We get so caught up with living that we forget why we have life. We forget the goodness of the Lord. We take breathing for granted. We take sight, hearing, walking, talking, etc., for granted. We proceed from day to day with business as usual. We need to stop every now and then to get a breath of fresh air. We need to reflect on God's amazing grace which is His unmerited favor to us. We need to realize whom we are leaning and depending on.

THE PROMISE

The LORD *is merciful and gracious, slow to anger, and plenteous in mercy. He will not always chide: neither will he keep his anger for ever. He hath not dealt with us after our sins; nor rewarded us according to our iniquities.*
Psalm 103:8-10 (KJV)

In Psalm 23 David reminded us that grace and

mercy shall follow us all the days of our lives.

Isn't that marvelous knowledge? We have the

grace and mercy of God with us each day.

Let's look at what Paul learned about God's grace.

And He has said to me, "My grace is sufficient for you, for
power is perfected in weakness." Most gladly, therefore, I
will rather boast about my weaknesses, so that the power of
Christ may dwell in me.
2 Corinthians 12:9 (NASB)

Awesome! Just awesome, that's what our God is.

God's grace is abundant. It's wonderful to know

that even in our weakest state God can use us.

Regardless of our situation we can find strength

from our Heavenly Father.

The power of Christ dwells in us always. Every day the Holy Spirit breathes on us.

Claim Check

Write a personal message to God about His promise to you.

*Because thou hast been my help, therefore
in the shadow of thy wings will I rejoice.*

Psalm 63:7 (KJV)

TOO BLESSED TO BE...

Dear Daughters,

Only you can fill in the blank. You and you alone know where God has bought you from. While man looks at the outside of a person, God looks inside at the soul. We can fool man by pretending to be something that we are not. We wear masks that hide our true person. We tend to seek approval at all costs, afraid to be the real us. If others could see the skeletons in some of our closets many of us would be shunned by society. There is a possibility that if some of the events of our past were made known they might make the headlines. As much as we try to hide our true selves, God sees all. He sees all and knows all. He sees all that we have been through. He sees all we've done. Every word spoken; every thought entertained is known by God. Despite our short comings God continues to bless us. Yes, I am truly too blessed to be…!

What about you?

THE PROMISE

Let all that I am praise the LORD; may I never forget the good things he does for me. He forgives all my sins and heals all my diseases. He redeems me from death and crowns me with love and tender mercies. He fills my life with good things. My youth is renewed like the eagle's!

Psalm 103:2-5(NLT)

BLESSED AND HIGHLY FAVORED

God loves us with an everlasting love. He loves us through our ups and downs or ins and outs. He loves us when we falter or step outside His will. He is a forgiving Father who does not stay angry forever. Worrying about our past, present or future state gets us nowhere. Worry is a tool of the enemy.

Let's look at Philippians 4:6, 7

Don't fret or worry. Instead of worrying, pray. Let petitions and praises shape your worries into prayers, letting God know your concerns. Before you know it, a sense of God's wholeness, everything coming together for good, will come and settle you down. It's wonderful what happens when Christ displaces worry at the center of your life.
Philippians 4:6 (MSG)

Paul tells the Philippians to turn their worries into prayers.

That is excellent advice. When the enemy is waging a war against us, we have to pray.

Turing everything over to God reminds us of how blessed we truly are.

Do you know that we are more than conquerors?

But in all these things we overwhelmingly conquer through Him who loved us.
Romans 8:37 (NASB)

????

Just what does that scripture mean?

In reading Romans 8 we discover the following facts. We are:

- Saved

- Loved

- Forgiven

- Adopted

- Victorious

- Redeemed

- Reconciled

- Chosen

- Filled with the Holy Spirit

- Strengthened in weakness

Yes, we are blessed and highly favored!

Claim Check

Write a personal message to God about His promise to you.

Then he said unto them, Go your way, eat the fat, and drink the sweet, and send portions unto them for whom nothing is prepared: for this day is holy unto our LORD: neither be ye sorry; for the joy of the LORD is your strength.

Nehemiah 8:10 (KJV)

STRENGTH NOT YOUR OWN

Dear Daughters,

What seems easy to some can often be unbearable for others? We all must learn to deal with circumstances in our life. We have a choice of crawling under the covers and burying our heads or we can look for the strength we need to face any situation.

One of Satan's tactics is to confront us when we seem to be at our lowest state. The truth is our strength comes from God not ourselves. God wants us to lean and depend on Him. His Word says that He can use a "contrite heart." We need to stop depending on earthly means of handling things and reach out for God. We feel defeated only when we try to do things by ourselves. We were not made for that. We can count on the Holy Spirit to provide everything we need to live from day to day. Remember that God is our strength and our help always.

THE PROMISE

But God hath revealed them unto us by his Spirit: for the Spirit searcheth all things, yea, the deep things of God.
1 Corinthians 2:10(KJV)

The Holy Spirit came to live in us the moment we

accepted Jesus as our personal Savior. He is here to

guide us from earth to Heaven.

Read the following scriptures to see how the Holy

Spirit is working with us.

*But the Comforter, which is the Holy Ghost, whom the
Father will send in my name, he shall teach you all things,
and bring all things to your remembrance, whatsoever I have
said unto you. John 14:26 (KJV)*

*Howbeit when he, the Spirit of truth, is come, he will guide
you into all truth: for he shall not speak of himself; but
whatsoever he shall hear, that shall he speak: and he will
shew you things to come. John 16:13 (KJV)*

*As they ministered to the Lord, and fasted, the Holy Ghost
said, Separate me Barnabas and Saul for the work
whereunto I have called them.
Acts 13:2 (KJV)*

*In the same way the Spirit also helps our weakness; for we
do not know how to pray as we should, but the Spirit
Himself intercedes for us with groanings too deep for words.
Romans 8:26 (NASB)*

**Praise God for His counseling, teaching,
guiding, speaking, and strengthening
us through the power of the Holy Spirit.**

Claim Check

Write a personal message to God about His promise to you.

*L*OR*D is thy shade upon thy right hand.*

The sun shall not smite thee by day, nor the moon by night.

Psalm 121:5-6 (KJV)

READY! SET! GO!

Dear Daughters,

On your mark, get ready, set, and go. Many races begin with the announcing of these words. Though not announced in this manner our journey with the Lord begins with getting ready. How? We accomplish this by surrendering ourselves to the Lord; by laying our ALL on the altar. We must allow the Lord to prepare us for the race. HOW? We must set our mind on God and His powers and provisions. Prayer and meditation are part of our preparation. We need to be in constant contact with the Lord. We must spend time with Him daily. Before our feet touch the floor, we should be starting our day with thankfulness. Our first thought should be of our Lord and Savior. Next, we should spend time studying and meditating on His Word. Once we learn the promises of God found in His Word it's harder for the enemy to deceive us. It's when we allow ourselves to become spiritually malnourished that we experience the enemy attacks more fiercely. The scripture says that the truth will set us free. Free to enjoy a wonderful fellowship with God. The truth of who we are and what God wants for us is found in His Word.

READY, SET, GO!!!!

Go where? Go to where the race leads. It leads to a life of service, a life of directions from the Lord. We can have a life of being God's child and enjoying a relationship that is truly indescribable if we continue to lean and depend on the Lord.

THE PROMISE

Therefore, since we have so great a cloud of witnesses surrounding us, let us also lay aside every encumbrance and the sin which so easily entangles us, and let us run with endurance the race that is set before us, ²fixing our eyes on Jesus, the author and perfecter of faith, who for the joy set before Him endured the cross, despising the shame, and has sat down at the right hand of the throne of God.

Hebrews 12:1-2(NASB)

RUNNING with GRACE

The following definitions were noted by Merriam-Webster as the meaning of grace:

A: unmerited divine assistance given humans for their regeneration or sanctification by a virtue coming from God
 A state of sanctification enjoyed through divine grace

For us to run the race set before us we need God's grace.

According to God's Word what does God's grace do for us?

By grace we are:

Saved   Eph. 2:8-9(NASB) *For by grace you have been saved through faith; and that not of yourselves, it is the gift of God; not as a result of works, so that no one may boast.*

Forgiven Isa. 43:25(NASB) I, *even I, am the one who wipes out your transgressions for My own sake, And I will not remember your sins.*

Sustained Phil. 2:13(NASB*) For it is God who is at work in you, both to will and to work for His good pleasure.*

Healed Ps. 147:3(NASB) He *heals the brokenhearted, and binds up their wounds.*

Liberated Mt. 11:28-30(NASB) *"Come to Me, all who are weary and heavy-laden, and I will give you rest. [29] Take My yoke upon you and learn from Me, for I am gentle and humble in heart, and YOU WILL FIND REST FOR YOUR SOULS. [30] For My yoke is easy and My burden is light."*

Given talents Rom. 12:6-8(NASB) *Since we have gifts that differ according to the grace given to us, each of us is to exercise them accordingly: if prophecy, according to the proportion of his faith; [7] if service, in* *his serving; or he who teaches, in his teaching; ⁸ or he who exhorts, in his exhortation; he who gives, with liberality; he who leads, with diligence; he who shows mercy, with cheerfulness.*

Used   **Eph. 3:7(KJV)** *Whereof I was made a minister, according to the gift of the grace of God given unto me by the effectual working of his power.*

Kept   **Jude 1:24**(NASB) Now *to Him who is able to keep you from stumbling, and to make you stand in the presence of His glory blameless with great joy.*

Transformed   **Rom. 12:2(NASB) And** *do not be conformed to this world, but be transformed by the renewing of your mind, so that you may prove what the will of God is, that which is good and acceptable and perfect.*

Matured   **2 Peter 3:18(NASB)** *But grow in the grace and knowledge of our Lord and Savior Jesus Christ. To Him be the glory, both now and to the day of eternity. Amen.*

We are blessed to have God's unmerited favor.

God's Amazing Grace

God's

Riches

At

Christ's

Expense

Claim Check

Write a personal message to God about His promise to you.

Therefore, let us draw near with confidence to the throne of grace, so that we may receive mercy and find grace to help in time of need.
Hebrews 4:16 (NASB)

STOP! BE STILL

Dear Daughters,

Quick, hurry, get moving, no time, can't stop, and keep pushing, faster, faster, faster. These words often characterize the pace of our lives. We must keep up the pace or we are subject to be left behind. We must be in the top 10% or we won't be recognized. We must meet certain social standards, or we won't measure up. We must forge ahead, or we'll end up nowhere. There's no time to waste. Papers must be written, meals must be prepared, and tasks must be completed. There just isn't enough time. Every minute of the day is full of action. Unless we keep the pace, we are doomed to a life of failure. These thoughts invade our minds until one day we realize that we can't move. We have followed all the formulas. We have taken all the suggestions from every magazine that we've read. We played by the rules, but we don't seem to be on top of things. Something seems to be missing. All our efforts seem in vain. What's wrong? Why isn't the path we are on leading to our desired outcomes? What do I do now? **NOTHING!** "Be still and know that I am God", is the message. To accomplish our goals we often fail to stop and ask for directions. We leave our guide on the side of the road and travel on by ourselves, only to discover that we are lost. We have no idea of which way to go. It is at this moment we realize that we have forgotten the most important element, GOD. Unless God directs our path, our journey is destined to lead nowhere.

Instead of trying to keep up with the world we ought to slow down and walk with the Lord. He will determine the pace for us. "Seek ye first the kingdom of God and all His righteousness" and He will put us on the right path.

THE PROMISE

*But seek ye first His kingdom and His
righteousness and all these things will be
added to you.*
Matthew 6:33

FOLLOW THE LEADER

Following God should be our top priority. In Matthew we are told to seek ye first the kingdom of God. Leaning and depending of God involves surrendering our total self.

We can leave nothing to chance. ***I hope, perhaps, maybe***, is the reasoning that some people use to decide their course of action. We don't have to pay Russian roulette with our lives.

Matthew 6:30-33

The Message (MSG)

30-33 "*If God gives such attention to the appearance of wildflowers—most of which are never even seen—don't you think he'll attend to you, take pride in you, do his best for you? What I'm trying to do here is to get you to relax, to not be so preoccupied with getting, so you can respond to God's giving. People who don't know God and the way he works fuss over these things, but you know both God and how he works. Steep your life in God-reality, God-initiative, God-provisions. Don't worry about missing out. You'll find all your everyday human concerns will be met.*

Claim Check

Write a personal message to God about

His promise to you.

Serve the LORD with gladness: come before his presence with singing.

Psalm 100:2 (KJV)

STANDING ON GOD'S PROMISES

God's Word is full of promises for all of us. Spending time in God's Word will give us the opportunity to learn how to lean and depend on the Lord. We are to renew our minds daily by thinking thoughts like Jesus. In the Word of God, we are told to have the mind of Christ in us. Christ focused on the mission that He came to earth to complete. He was about his Father's business. We like Christ have a purpose. Our purpose is to do the will of God.

PROMISES

John 6:47

*Verily, verily, I say unto you, He that believeth
on me hath everlasting life.*

Romans 10:9

*That if thou shalt confess with thy mouth the
Lord Jesus, and shalt believe I thine heart that
God hath raised him from the dead, thou shalt
be saved.*

Psalm 86:5

*For thou, Lord, art good, and ready to forgive;
and plenteous in mercy unto all them that call
upon thee.*

Romans 5:8

But God commendeth his love toward us, in that, while we were yet sinners, Christ died for us.

John 3:16

For God so loved the world that he gave his only begotten Son, that whosoever believeth in him should not perish, but have everlasting life.

Romans 8:38,39

For I am persuaded, that neither death, nor life, nor angels, nor principalities, nor powers, nor things, present, nor things to come. Nor height, nor depth, nor any other creature, shall be able to separate us from the love of God, which is in Christ Jesus our Lord.

Isaiah 26:3

Thou wilt keep him in perfect peace, whose mind is stayed on thee: because he trusteth in thee.

Psalm 29:11

The Lord will give strength unto his people; the Lord will bless his people with peace.

Philippians 4:6, 7

Be careful for nothing, but in everything by prayer and supplication with thanksgiving let your request be made known unto God. And the peace of God, which passesth all understanding, shall keep your hearts and minds through Christ Jesus.

II Corinthians 5:21

For he hath made him to be sin for us, who knew no sin; that we might be made the righteousness of God in him.

Revelation 3:20

Behold , I stand at the door, and knock: if any man hear my voice, and open the door, I will come in to him, and will sup with him, and he with me.

Matthew 18:20

For where two or three are gathered together in my name, there am I in the midst of them.

Isaiah 43:2

When thou passest through the waters, I will be with thee; and though the rivers, they shall not overflow thee; when thou walkest through the fire, thou shalt not be burned; neither shall the flame kindle upon thee.

Philippians 1:6

Being confident of this very thing, that he which hath begun a good work in you will perform it until the day of Jesus Christ.

Psalm 23:6

Surely goodness and mercy shall follow e all the days of my glife and I will dwell in the house of the Lord for ever.

II Corinthians 9:8

And God is able to make all grace abound toward you; that, ye, always having all sufficiency in all things, may abound to every good work.

Philippians 4:19

But my God shall supply all you need according to his riches in glory by Christ Jesus.

Psalm 103:2-4

Bless the Lord, O my soul, and forget not all his benefits; Who forgiveth all thine iniquities; who healeth all diseases; who redeemeth thy life from destruction; who crowneth thee with lovingkindness and tender mercies.

John 6:35

And Jesus said unto them, I am the bread of life; he that cometh to me shall never hunger; and he that believeth on me shall never thirst.

II Timothy 3:16

All Scripture is given by inspiration of God, and is profitable for doctrine, for reproof, for correction, for instruction in righteousness.

I Corinthians 2:9

But as it is written, Eye hath not seen, nor ear heard, neither have entered into the heart of man, the things which God hath prepared for them that love him.

Psalm 32:8

I will instruct thee and teach thee in the way which thiu shalt go: I will guide thee with mine eye.

Matthew 24:35

Heaven and earth shall pass away, but my .

words shall not

Isaiah 40:31

But they that wait upon the Lord shall renew their strength; they shall mount up with wings as eagles; they shall run, and not be weary; and they shall walk, and not faint.

Isaiah 26:3

Thou wilt keep him in perfect peace, whose mind is stayed on thee, because he trusteth in thee.

Hebrews 13:5

Let your conversation be without covetousness; and be content with such things as ye have: for he hath said, I will never leave thee, nor forsake thee.

Isaiah 41:10

Fear thou not; for I am with thee: be not dismayed; for I am thy God: I will strengthen thee: ye, I will help thee: yea, I will uphold thee with the right hand of my righteousness.

John 14:18

I will not leave you comfortless: I will come to you.

Psalm 147:3

He healeth the broken in heart, and bindeth up their wounds.

Deuteronomy 31:6

Be strong and of a good courage, fear not, nor be afraid of them: for the Lord thy God, he it is the doth go with thee; he will not fail, thee nor forsake thee.

II Corinthians 5:17

Therefore if any man be in Christ, he is a new creature, old things are passed away; behold all things are become new.

I Corinthians 14:33

For God is not the author of confusion, but of peace, as in all churches of the saints

Isaiah 50:7

For the Lord God will help me; therefore shall I not be confounded; therefore have I set my face like a flint, and I know that I shall not be ashamed.

Psalm 32:8

I will instruct thee and teach thee in the way which thou shalt go: I will guide thee with mine eye.

Psalm 55:22

Cast thy burden upon the Lord, and he shall sustain thee: he shall never suffer the righteous to be moved.

I John 1:9

If we confess our sins, he is faithful and just to forgive us our sins, and to cleanse us from all unrighteousness.

James 4:7

Submit yourselves to God. Resist the devil , and he will flee from you.

I Peter 1:6, 7

Wherein ye greatly rejoice, though now for a season, if need be, ye are in heaviness through manifold temptations. That the trial of your faith, being much more precious than of gold that perisheth, though it be tried with fire, might be found unto praise and honour and glory and the appearing of Jesus Christ.

Matthew 6:14

For if ye forgive men their trespasses, your heavenly Father will also forgive you.

II Timothy 1:7

For God has not given us the spirit of fear, but of power, and love, and of a sound mind.

Psalm 56:11

In God have I put my trust: I will not be afraid what man can do unto me.

John 14:27

Peace I leave with you, my peace I give unto you: not as the world giveth, give I unto you. Let not your heart be troubled, neither let it be afraid.

Psalm 27:14

Wait on the Lord: be of good courage, and he shall strengthen thine heart: wait, I say, on the Lord.

Romans 14:17-19

For the kingdom of God is not meat and drink; but righteousness, and peace, and joy in the Holy Ghost. For he that in these things serveth Christ is acceptable to God, and approved of men. Let us therefore follow after the things which make for peace, and things wherewith one may edify another.

John 14:21

He that hath my commandments, and keepth them, he it is that loveth me: and he that loveth me shall be loved of my Father, and I will love him, and will manifest myself to him.

John 3:16

For God so loved the world, that he gave his only begotten Son, that whosoever believeth in him should not perish, but have everlasting life.

John 6:47

Verily, verily, I say unto you. He that believeth on me hath everlasting life.

John 6:51

I am the living bread which came down from heaven: if any man eat of this bread, he shall live for ever: and the bread that I will give is my flesh, which I will give for the life of the world.

Exodus 23:25, 26

An ye shall serve the Lord your God, and he sall bless thy bread, and thy water:and I will take sickness away from the midst of thee. There shall notung cast their young, nor be baren. In thy land: the number of your days I will fufil.

Psalm 84:11

For the Lord God is a sun and shield: the Lord will give grace and glory: no good thing will he withhold from then that walk uprightly.

Hebrews 4:16

Let us therefore come boldly unto the throne of grace, that we may obtain mercy, and find grace to help in time of need.

John 14:16, 17

And I will pray the Father, and he shall give you another Comforter, that he may abide with you for ever; Even the Spirit of truth; whom the world cannot receive, because it seeth him not, neither knoweth him; but ye know him; for he dwelleth with you, and shall be in you.

John 16:7, 13

Howbeit when he, the Spirit of truth, is come, he will guide you into all truth: for he shall not speak of himself; but whatsoever he shall hear, that shall he speak: and he will shew you things to come.

Genesis 9:16

And the bow shall be in the cloud, and I will look upon it, that I may remember that everlasting covenant between God and every living creature of all flesh that is upon the earth,

II Peter 3:9

The Lord is not slack concerning his promise, as some men count slackness; but is longsuffering to us-ward, not willing that any should perish, but that all should come to repentance.

Job 36:11

If they obey and serve him, they shall spend their days in prosperity, and their years in pleasure.

Matthew 6:14, 15

For if ye forgive men their trespasses, your heavenly Father will also forgive you: but if ye forgive not men their trespasses, neither will your Father forgive your trespasses.

Psalm 119:115

Thy word is a lamp unto my feet, and a light unto my path.

Proverbs 16:3

Commit thy works unto the Lord, and thy thoughts shall be established.

Psalm 37:23

The steps of a good man are ordered by the Lord; and he delighteth in his way.

Isaiah 65:24

And it shall come to pass, that before they call, I will answer;and while they are yet speaking, I will hear.

Psalm 37:4

Delight thyself also in the Lord; and he shall give thee the desires of thine heart.

Psalm 91:15

He shall call upon me, and I will answer hin: I will be with him in trouble; I will deliver him, and honour him.

Jeremiah 33:3

Call unto me, and I will answer thee, and shew thee great and mighty things, which thou knowest not.

Proverbs 3:5, 6

Trust in the Lord with all thine heart; and lean not unto thine own understanding. In all thy ways acknowledge him, and he shall direct thy paths.

About the Author

Bonita Williams, a generational author, is a servant of God, whose passion is spreading the news of the gospel of Jesus Christ with all she meets. Her greatest desire is to utilize her God given gifts to make a positive difference in the lives of others. She is a Bible teacher, workshop facilitator, empowerment seminar leader, and a conference speaker who has committed her life to instructing, inspiring, and encouraging women of faith. Bonita and her husband Benny reside in Atlanta where they are in service to the Lord.

Reflections

Reflections

Reflections

Reflections

Reflections

Reflections

Reflections

Reflections

The Iphigenia in Tauris by Euripedes

Euripides is rightly lauded as one of the great dramatists of all time. In his lifetime, he wrote over 90 plays and although only 18 have survived they reveal the scope and reach of his genius.

Euripides is identified with many theatrical innovations that have influenced drama all the way down to modern times, especially in the representation of traditional, mythical heroes as ordinary people in extraordinary circumstances.

As would be expected from a life lived 2,500 years ago, details of it are few and far between. Accounts of his life, written down the ages, do exist but whether much is reliable or surmised is open to debate.

Most accounts agree that he was born on Salamis Island around 480 BC, to mother Cleito and father Mnesarchus, a retailer who lived in a village near Athens. Upon the receipt of an oracle saying that his son was fated to win "crowns of victory", Mnesarchus insisted that the boy should train for a career in athletics.

However, what is clear is that athletics was not to be the way to win crowns of victory. Euripides had been lucky enough to have been born in the era as the other two masters of Greek Tragedy; Sophocles and Æschylus. It was in their footsteps that he was destined to follow.

His first play was performed some thirteen years after the first of Socrates plays and a mere three years after Æschylus had written his classic The Oristria.

Theatre was becoming a very important part of the Greek culture. The Dionysia, held annually, was the most important festival of theatre and second only to the fore-runner of the Olympic games, the Panathenia, held every four years, in appeal.

Euripides first competed in the City Dionysia, in 455 BC, one year after the death of Æschylus, and, incredibly, it was not until 441 BC that he won first prize. His final competition in Athens was in 408 BC. The Bacchae and Iphigenia in Aulis were performed after his death in 405 BC and first prize was awarded posthumously. Altogether his plays won first prize only five times.

Euripides was also a great lyric poet. In Medea, for example, he composed for his city, Athens, "the noblest of her songs of praise". His lyric skills however are not just confined to individual poems: "A play of Euripides is a musical whole....one song echoes motifs from the preceding song, while introducing new ones."

Much of his life and his whole career coincided with the struggle between Athens and Sparta for hegemony in Greece but he didn't live to see the final defeat of his city.

Euripides fell out of favour with his fellow Athenian citizens and retired to the court of Archelaus, king of Macedon, who treated him with consideration and affection.

At his death, in around 406BC, he was mourned by the king, who, refusing the request of the Athenians that his remains be carried back to the Greek city, buried him with much splendor within his own dominions. His tomb was placed at the confluence of two streams, near Arethusa in Macedonia, and a cenotaph was built to his memory on the road from Athens towards the Piraeus.

Index of Contents

The Iphigenia in Tauris is not in the modern sense a tragedy; it is a romantic play, beginning in a tragic atmosphere and moving through perils and escapes to a happy end. To the archaeologist the cause of this lies in the ritual on which the play is based. All Greek tragedies that we know have as their nucleus something which the Greeks called an Aition—a cause or origin. They all explain some ritual or observance or commemorate some great event. Nearly all, as a matter of fact, have for this Aition a Tomb Ritual, as, for instance, the Hippolytus has the worship paid by the Trozenian Maidens at that hero's grave. The use of this Tomb Ritual may well explain both the intense shadow of death that normally hangs over the Greek tragedies, and also perhaps the feeling of the Fatality, which is, rightly or wrongly, supposed to be prominent in them. For if you are actually engaged in commemorating your hero's funeral, it follows that all through the story, however bright his prospects may seem, you feel that he is bound to die; he cannot escape. A good many tragedies, however, are built not on Tomb Rituals but on other sacred Aitia: on the foundation of a city, like the Aetnae, the ritual of the torch- race, like the Prometheus; on some great legendary succouring of the oppressed, like the Suppliant Women of Aeschylus and Euripides. And the rite on which the Iphigenia is based is essentially one in which a man is brought to the verge of death but just does not die.

The rite is explained in the play. On a certain festival at Halae in Attica a human victim was led to the altar of Artemis Tauropolos, touched on the throat with a sword and then set free: very much what happened to Orestes among the Tauri, and exactly what happened to Iphigenia at Aulis. Both legends have doubtless grown out of the same ritual.

Like all the great Greek legends, the Iphigenia myths take many varying forms. They are all of them, in their essence, conjectural restorations, by poets or other 'wise men,' of supposed early history. According to the present play, Agamemnon, when just about to sail with all the powers of Greece against Troy, was bound by weather at Aulis. The medicine-man Calchas explained that Artemis demanded the sacrifice of his daughter, Iphigenia, who was then at home with her mother, Clytemnestra. Odysseus and Agamemnon sent for the maiden on the pretext that she was to be married to the famous young hero, Achilles; she was brought to Aulis and treacherously slaughtered—or, at least, so people thought.

There is a subject for tragedy there; and it was brilliantly treated in Euripides' Iphigenia in Aulis, which was probably left unfinished at his death. But our play chooses a later moment of the story.

In reality Artemis at the last moment saved Iphigenia, rapt her away from mortal eyes and set her down in the land of the Tauri to be her priestess. (In Tauris is only the Latin for "among the Tauri.") These Tauri possessed an image of Artemis which had fallen from heaven, and kept up a savage rite of sacrificing to it all strangers who were cast on their shores. Iphigenia, obedient to her goddess, and held by "the spell of the altar," had to consecrate the victims as they went in to be slain. So far only barbarian strangers had come: she waited half in horror, half in a rage of revenge, for the day when she should have to sacrifice a Greek. The first Greek that came was her own brother, Orestes, who had been sent by Apollo to take the image of Artemis and bear it to Attica, where it should no more be stained with human sacrifice.

If we try to turn from these myths to the historical facts that underlay them, we may conjecture that there were three goddesses of the common Aegean type, worshipped in different places. At Brauron and elsewhere there was Iphigenia ('Birth-mighty'); at Halae there was the Tauropolos ('the Bull-rider,' like Europa, who rode on the horned Moon); among the savage and scarcely known Tauri there was some goddess to whom shipwrecked strangers were sacrificed. Lastly there came in the Olympian Artemis. Now all these goddesses (except possibly the Taurian, of whom we know little) were associated with the Moon and with child-birth, and with rites for sacrificing or redeeming the first-born. Naturally enough, therefore, they were all gradually absorbed by the prevailing worship of Artemis. Tauropolis became an epithet of Artemis, Iphigenia became her priestess and 'Keybearer.' And the word 'Tauropolis,' which had become obscure, was explained as a reference to the Tauri. The old rude image of Tauropolis had come from the Tauri, and the strange ritual was descended from their bloody rites. So the Taurian goddess must be Artemis too. The tendency of ancient polytheism, when it met with some alien religion, was not to treat the alien gods as entirely new persons, but assuming the real and obvious existence of their own gods, to inquire by what names and with what ritual the strangers worshipped them.

As usual in Euripides, the central character of this play is a woman, and a woman most unsparingly yet lovingly studied. Iphigenia is no mere 'sympathetic heroine.' She is a worthy member of her great but sinister house; a haggard and exiled woman, eating out her heart in two conflicting emotions: intense longing for home and all that she had loved in childhood, and bitter self-pitying rage against 'her murderers.' The altar of Aulis is constantly in her thoughts. She does not know whether to hate her father, but at least she can with a clear conscience hate all the rest of those implicated, Calchas, Odysseus, Menelaus, and most fiercely, though somewhat unjustly, Helen. All the good women in Euripides go wild at the name of Helen. Iphigenia broods on her wrongs till she can see nothing else; she feels as if she hated all Greeks, and lived only for revenge, for the hope of some day slaughtering Greeks at her altar, as pitilessly as they slaughtered her at Aulis. She knows how horrible this state of mind is, but she is now "turned to stone, and has no pity left in her." Then the Greeks come; and even before she knows who they really are, the hard shell of her bitterness slowly yields. Her heart goes out to them; she draws Orestes against his will into talk; she insists on pitying him, insists on his pitying her; and eventually determines, come what may, that she will save at least the one stranger that she has talked with most. Presently comes the discovery who the strangers are; and she is at once ready to die with them or for them.

As for the scene in which Iphigenia befools Thoas, my moral feelings may be obtuse, but I certainly cannot feel the slightest compunction or shock at the heavy lying. Which of us would not expect at least as much from his own sister, if it lay with her to save him from the altars of Benin or Ashanti? I suspect that the good people who lament over "the low standard of truthfulness shown by even the most enlightened pagans" have either forgotten the days when they read stories of adventure, or else have not, in reading this scene, realised properly the strain of hairbreadth peril that lies behind the comedy of it. A single slip in Iphigenia's tissue of desperate improvisations would mean death, and not to herself alone. One feels rather sorry for Thoas, certainly, and he is a very fine fellow in his way; but a person who insists on slaughtering strangers cannot expect those strangers or their friends to treat him with any approach to candour.

The two young men come nearer to mere ideal heroes de roman than any other characters in Euripides. They are surprisingly handsome and brave and unselfish and everything that they should be; and they stand out like heroes against the mob of cowardly little Taurians in the Herdsman's speech. Yet they have none of the unreality that is usual in such figures. The shadow of madness and guilt hanging over Orestes makes a difference. At his first entrance, when danger is still far off, he is a mass of broken nerves; he depends absolutely on Pylades. In the later scenes, when they are face to face with death, the underlying strength of the son of the Great King asserts itself and makes one understand why, for all his madness, Orestes is the chief, and Pylades only the devoted follower.

Romantic plays with happy endings are almost of necessity inferior in artistic value to true tragedies. Not, one would hope, simply because they end happily; happiness in itself is certainly not less beautiful than grief; but because a tragedy in its great moments can generally afford to be sincere, while romantic plays live in an atmosphere of ingenuity and make-believe. The Iphigenia is not of the same order as The Trojan Women. Yet it is a delightful play; subtle, ever-changing, full of movement and poignancy. The recognition scene became to Aristotle a model of what such a scene should be; and the long passage before it, from the entrance of the two princes onward, seems to me one of the most skilful and fascinating in Greek drama.

And after all the adventure of Euripides is not quite like that of the average romantic writer. It is shot through by reflection, by reality and by sadness. There is a shadow that broods over the Iphigenia, though it is not the shadow of death. It is exile, homesickness. Iphigenia, Orestes, the Women of the Chorus, are all exiles, all away from their heart's home, among savage people and cruel gods. They wait on the shore while the sea-birds take wing for Hellas, out beyond the barrier of the Dark-Blue Rocks and the great stretches of magical and 'unfriended' sea. Nearly all the lyrics are full of sea-light and the clash of waters, and the lyrics are usually the very soul of Euripidean tragedy.

Gilbert Murray

THE PERSONS

IPHIGENIA, eldest daughter of Agamemnon, King of Argos; supposed to have been sacrificed by him to Artemis at Aulis.
ORESTES, her brother; pursued by Furies for killing his mother, Clytemnestra, who had murdered Agamemnon.
PYLADES, Prince of Phocis, friend to Orestes.
THOAS, King of Tauris, a savage country beyond the Symplegades.
A HERDSMAN
A MESSENGER
CHORUS of Captive Greek Women, handmaids to Iphigenia.
The Goddess PALLAS ATHENA.

FIRST PERFORMED